ARTIST TRANSCRIPTIONS®
TRUMPET

The Dizzy Gillespie Collection

Transcriptions by Kobi Arad and Timo Shanko

Cover Photo courtesy of Institute of Jazz Studies

ISBN 0-634-01760-8

7777 W. Bluemound Rd. P.O. Box 13819 Milwaukee, WI 53213

Visit Hal Leonard Online at
www.halleonard.com

Of all the luminaries in jazz, Dizzy Gillespie was among the most significant. Along with fellow 1940s modernists including drummer Kenny Clarke, pianist Thelonious Monk, and alto saxophonist Charlie Parker, Gillespie codified bebop—a language that today represents the common practice of jazz. With his signature look—beret, goatee, and horn-rimmed glasses—and an equally sharp elocution, Gillespie was, in fact, the archetypal bebopper. While colleagues preferred to be enigmatic, Gillespie enthusiastically explained his innovations to budding jazzers, thereby helping to cement the music's posterity.

Born into an impoverished South Carolina family in 1917, John Birks Gillespie received a rudimentary musical education from his father, who was an amateur bandleader. Starting on trombone, then switching to trumpet in his teens, Gillespie received a scholarship to North Carolina's Laurinburg Institute, where he studied harmony and theory while independently sharpening his trumpet and piano skills.

Gillespie withdrew from school in 1935, then joined Frankie Fairfax's band in Philadelphia. There, on account of his penchant for pranks, Gillespie earned the nickname "Dizzy." In 1937, Gillespie enlisted in Teddy Hill's band, where he filled a slot vacated by trumpeter Roy Eldridge, a personal benchmark. Gillespie was a featured soloist in Cab Calloway's orchestra from 1939-1941. During that tenure, Gillespie's extemporizations—especially on "Pickin' the Cabbage"—began to reveal an uncanny harmonic sense, foreshadowing bebop innovations. Nevertheless, Calloway condescended to Gillespie, labeling his experiments "Chinese music." An infamous spitball incident—in which Gillespie was mistakenly identified as the shooter—resulted in the trumpeter's dismissal from the group.

In the early 1940s, Gillespie freelanced with the bands of Benny Carter, Ella Fitzgerald, Coleman Hawkins, and others, participating in a handful of seminal sessions. With Carter in 1942, Gillespie penned what was to become his most famous composition ("A Night in Tunisia"), and with Hawkins, the trumpeter wrote and recorded "Woodyn' You" (1944)—a composition commonly believed to have represented the first iteration of bebop.

During the early- to mid-1940s, Gillespie—full of ideas—participated in late night jam sessions at Minton's Playhouse in Harlem, where he, Kenny Clarke, Thelonious Monk, Charlie Parker, and assorted others developed bebop. Gillespie and Parker began recording sides for the Musicraft, Guild, and Savoy labels, confounding swing fans with advanced numbers like "Groovin' High," "Salt Peanuts," and "Shaw 'Nuff."

After leading and touring with an unsuccessful big band in 1945, Gillespie returned to New York and assembled a heavyweight orchestra and workshop, through which John Coltrane, future members of the Modern Jazz Quartet, and Chano Pozo would pass. In his new big band, Gillespie began experimenting with Latin music. The trumpeter's composition "Manteca," written with percussionist Pozo and arranger Gil Fuller, fused jazz with Afro-Cuban music, marking the creation of an appealing new language. Through a contract with RCA Records, Gillespie's groundbreaking big band enjoyed prosperity until 1950, when economic problems necessitated its disbanding.

In a serendipitous 1953 accident, Gillespie's trumpet was bent upward; he preferred the new sound, and played custom-deformed horns thereafter. Gillespie's bent horn and puffed-out cheeks would become one of jazz's most iconic images.

In 1956, the US State Department funded a new big band for Gillespie, and with hot young sidemen—including saxophonist Benny Golson, trumpeter Lee Morgan, and pianist Wynton Kelly—he toured overseas extensively. This arrangement was especially significant in that it marked the first time the US government gave recognition and pecuniary assistance to jazz. Gillespie's second big band split up in 1958, though, partly due to taxpayers' disapproval of funding a jazz group.

Gillespie fronted various small ensembles throughout the 1960s, leading such sidemen as reed player James Moody, pianists Kenny Barron and Junior Mance, and bassist Chuck Rainey. During that decade, Gillespie also enjoyed unprecedented popularity; California devotees even placed him as an independent candidate for US President.

In 1968, Gillespie toured Europe with his Reunion Big Band, and in the early '70s, he participated in the worldwide Giants of Jazz tour, featuring, among others, fellow legend Thelonious Monk. By that time, Gillespie's technical prowess had begun to diminish. Regardless, he remained a foremost jazz ambassador—touring the world, tutoring young players, and recording a trove of albums for Pablo.

During his last years, Gillespie amassed numerous accolades, including a National Medal of the Arts (1989), a Kennedy Center Honor (1990), and twenty honorary degrees from institutions such as Columbia University and the New England Conservatory. In 1988 Gillespie initiated the United Nations Orchestra—an all-star big band including trumpeter Arturo Sandoval and reed player Paquito D'Rivera. Gillespie remained active until shortly before his 1993 passing.

—Adam Perlmutter

Contents

4 Anthropology *(Take 1)*
9 Anthropology *(Take 2)*
14 Blue 'n Boogie
18 Con Alma
24 Dizzy Atmosphere
29 Dizzy Meets Sonny
40 I Can't Get Started with You
43 It Don't Mean a Thing *(If It Ain't Got That Swing)*
52 Jambo
60 Jersey Bounce
64 Manteca
68 A Night in Tunisia
72 Rose Room
55 Salt Peanuts
74 Sophisticated Lady
80 Stardust
82 Stella by Starlight
77 Tin Tin Deo
94 Tour de Force
100 Woodyn' You

Discography

Notes:

1. Most of these recordings were first issued as singles during the 78rpm era, hence these are the first issues listed. Recordings made for such labels as Guild and Musicraft are now in the public domain, and have been issued on many CDs on a variety of labels.
2. The title marked with an "*" was recorded in France, and the LP issue reflects its initial U.S. release label and number.
3. Titles marked with a "+" are non-commercial recordings or broadcast airchecks. Only current CD issues are listed.

Anthropology:
  Take 1–78: RCA Victor 40-1032; Take 2–LP: RCA Victor LPV 530
  Both Takes–CD: Bluebird 66528
Blue 'n Boogie–78: Guild 1001; CD: Masters of Jazz MJCD 113
Con Alma–LP: Norgran MGN 1003; CD: Verve 314 513 875
Dizzy Atmosphere–78: Musicraft 488; CD: Masters of Jazz MJCD 121
Dizzy Meets Sonny (Modern Jazz Sextet)–LP: Norgran MGN 1076; CD: Verve
I Can't Get Started with You, Tour de Force–LP: Norgran MGN 1084; CD: Verve 314 527 900
It Don't Mean a Thing–LP: Norgran MGN 1050; CD: Verve
Jambo–LP: Limelight LS 86007; CD: Verve 557 492
Jersey Bounce (Les Hite and His Orchestra)–78: Hit; CD: Masters of Jazz MJCD 45
Manteca–78: RCA Victor 20-3023; CD: Bluebird 66528
+Rose Room (John Kirby and His Orchestra)–CD: Masters of Jazz MJCD 86
Salt Peanuts–78: Guild 1003; CD: Masters of Jazz MJCD 121
Sophisticated Lady–LP: Verve V6 8386; CD: Verve 817 107
+Stardust–CD: Masters of Jazz MJCD 45
*Stella by Starlight–LP: Prestige; CD: Verve 159 734
Tin Tin Deo–78: Dee Gee 3601; CD: Savoy 78815
Woodyn' You–78: Apollo; CD: Delmar 459

Anthropology
(Take 1)

By Charlie Parker
and Dizzy Gillespie

A7
D13
G7
G7b5(b9)
C7
C7/E
Dm7
G7
C7
Am7
D7
G7b9
C9
F7b9
Fm7
C7
C7
VIBES SOLO
31
C7
C7/E
Dm7
D#°7
C7
A7b13
D7
G7b9
F7
F#°7
C/G
G7

6
C7
C/E
Dm7
G7
C7
Am7
D7
G7b9
C7
F7
C/G
G7
C7
E7b9(b13)
A7#11
D13
G7
G7b5(b9)
C7
C7/E
Dm7
G7
C7
Am7

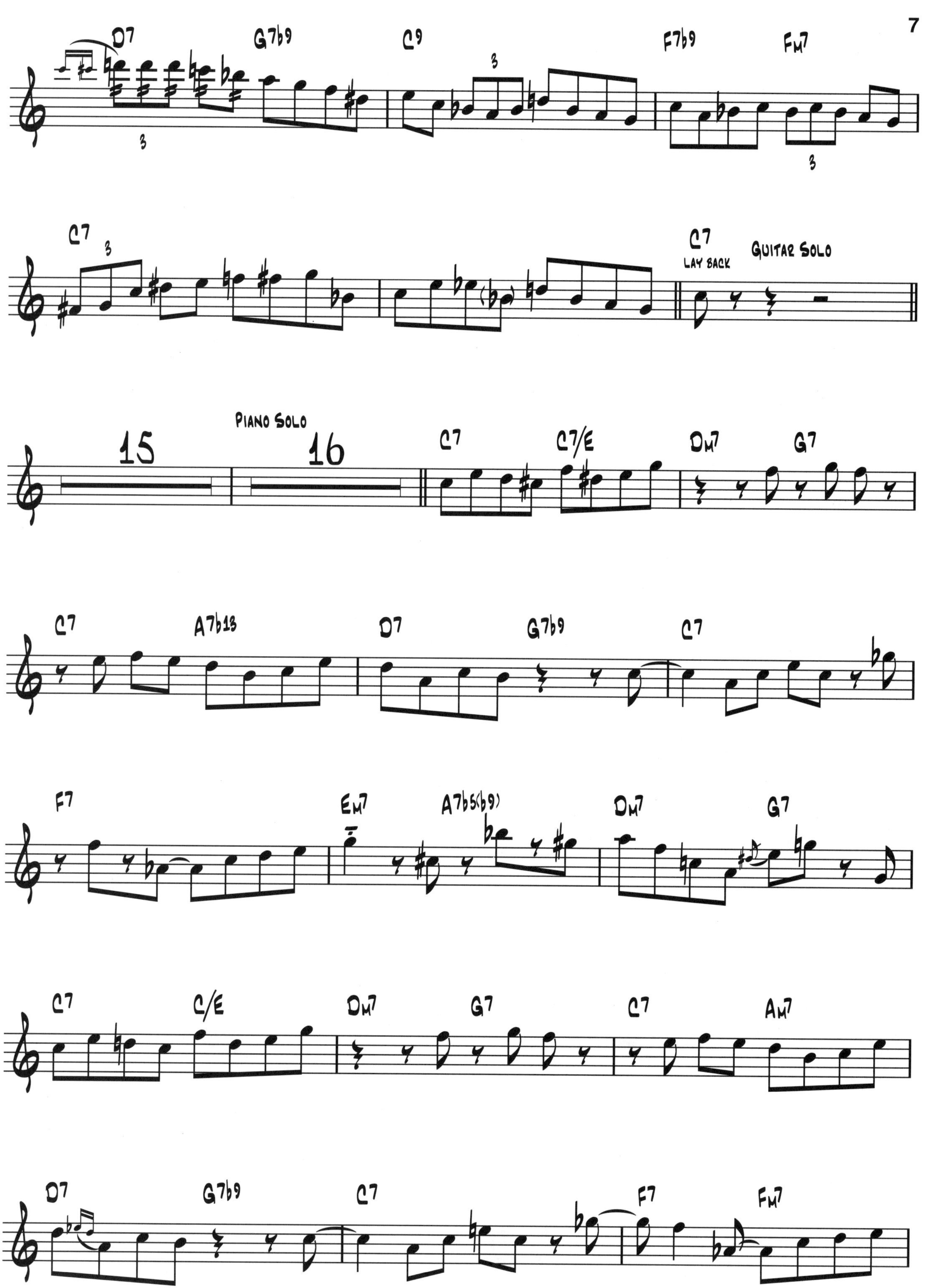
D7
G7♭9
C9
F7♭9
FM7
C7
C7
LAY BACK
GUITAR SOLO
15
PIANO SOLO
16
C7
C7/E
DM7
G7
C7
A7♭13
D7
G7♭9
C7
F7
EM7
A7♭5(♭9)
DM7
G7
C7
C/E
DM7
G7
C7
AM7
D7
G7♭9
C7
F7
FM7

F7♭9 Fm7 C7

Anthropology
(Take 2)

By Charlie Parker
and Dizzy Gillespie

A7
D13
G7b5(b9)
C7
C7/E
Dm7
G7b9
C7
A7b9(b13)
D7b9
G7b9
C7
F7
Fm13
C7/G
C7
VIBES SOLO
32
C7
C7/E
Dm7
D#o7
C7
A7b13
D7
G7b9
C9
F7
Fm7
Em7
G7#11
C7

Dm7
D#°7
C7
A7b9(b13)
D7b9
G7b5(b9)
C7
C7/E
Dm7
D#°7/F#
C7
E7b5(b9)
A7#11
D7
G9#11
C7
C7/E
Dm7
G7b9
C7
A7b9(b13)
D7b9
C7b9

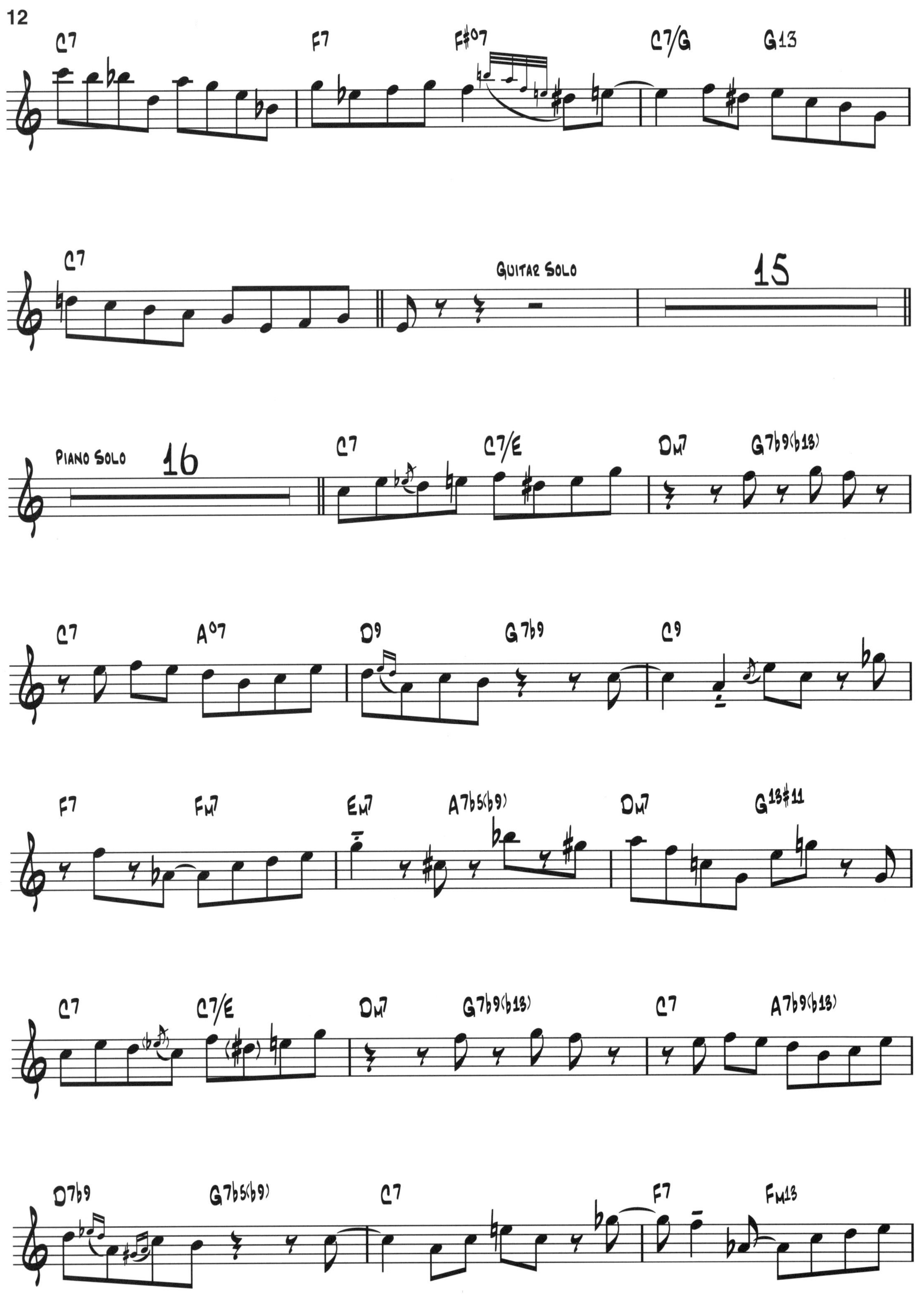
C7
F7
F#o7
C7/G
G13
C7
GUITAR SOLO
15
PIANO SOLO
16
C7
C7/E
Dm7
G7b9(b13)
C7
Ao7
D9
G7b9
C9
F7
Fm7
Em7
A7b5(b9)
Dm7
G13#11
C7
C7/E
Dm7
G7b9(b13)
C7
A7b9(b13)
D7b9
G7b5(b9)
C7
F7
Fm13

C7
E9♯11

A7

D13
G7♭5(♭9)

C7
C7/E
Dm7
G7♭9

C7
A7♭9(♭13)
D7♭9
G7♭9
C7

F7
Fm13
C7/G

BLUE 'N BOOGIE

BY JOHN "DIZZY" GILLESPIE
AND FRANK PAPARELLI

F7

C7 Dm7 G7

C7

PIANO SOLO 23

TRUMPET -- OPEN

TENOR

C7

BREAK

N.C.

F7

TENOR SOLO 18

DIZZY

C7

F7

C7

G7#5

C7
C7
F7
C7
Dm7
G7
C7
C7
False Fingering
F7
C7
Dm7
G7
C7

C7
F7
C7
Dm7
G7
C7
Guitar Solo
11
C7
Cup Mute
F7
C7
Dm7
G7
C7

Con Alma

By John "Dizzy" Gillespie

D
DM7b5
G7
AbM7
G7
F#
GM7
C7
Gb
Bb7/F
EbM
EbM7/Db
C7
F
FM7
E7
Eb
G7/D
CM
CM7/Bb
A7
DIZZY SOLO
D
Gb
Bb7/F
EbM
EbM7/Db
C7
F
FM7
E7
Eb
G7/D
CM
CM7/Bb

A7
D
Gb
Bb7/F
Ebm
Ebm7/Db
C7
3
F
Fm7
E7
3
Eb
G7/D
Cm
Cm7/Bb
A7
3
3
D
Dm7b5
G7
G#m7
3
C#7
F#
3
3
3
Gm7
C7
3
Gb
Bb7/F
Ebm
Ebm7
C7
3

F
F7
E7
Eb
G7/D
Cm
Cm7/Bb
A7
D
PIANO
15
DIZZY
Dm7b5
G7
Abm7
Db7
G7
Gb
Gm7
C7
Gb
Bb7/F
Ebm
Ebm7/Db
C7
F
Fm7
E7

Eb G7/D Cm Cm7/Bb
A7 D Gb Bb7/F
Ebm Ebm7/Db C7
F Fm7 E7 Eb G7/D
Cm Cm7/Bb A7 D
Gb Bb/F Ebm Ebm7/Db C7
F F7 E7 Eb G7/D
Cm Cm7/Bb A7

D
Dm7b5
G7
Abm7
G7
Gb
Gm7
C7
Gb
Bb7/F
Ebm
Ebm7/Db
C7
F
Fm7
E7
Eb
G7/D
Cm
Cm7/Bb
A7
D
D7#9
Gm

Dizzy Atmosphere

By John "Dizzy" Gillespie

Eb13
D13
Db13
C13
B13
Bb
GM7
CM7
F7
Bb
GM7
CM7
F7
Bb7
Eb
Bb
BIRD SOLO
30
DIZZY SOLO
OPEN
Bb
G7
C7
F7
DM7
G7
CM7
F7
Bb7

Eb
Bb
Bb
Gm7
Cm7
F7
Bb
Gm7
Cm7
F7
Bb
Eb
Bb
E7
Eb7
D7
Db7
C7
B7
Bb
G7
Cm7
F7
Bb
G7

CM7 F7 Bb7 Eb
Bb
BASS SOLO
31
CUP MUTE
Bb GM7 CM7 F7
Bb G7 CM7 F7 Bb7
Eb Bb
Bb GM7 CM7 F7 Bb GM7
CM7 F7 Bb7 Eb
Bb E7

Eb7
D7
Db7
C7#11
B7#11
Bb
Gm7
Cm7
F7
Bb
Gm7
Cm7
F7
Bb7
Eb
Bb
Bb/F
Bb

Dizzy Meets Sonny

By John "Dizzy" Gillespie

A7 D7
G7
C Dm7 G7 C
Dm7 G7 C7 F
C C Dm7 G7
C Dm7 G7 C7
F C
C Dm7 G7 C Dm7 G7

C7
F
C
E7
A7
D7
G7
C
Dm7
G7
C
Dm7
G7
C7
F
C
C
Dm7
G7
C
Dm7
G7
C7
F
C

C Dm7 G7
C Dm7 G7 C7 F
C E7
A7
D7 G7
C Dm7 G7
C Dm7 G7 C7
F C C

Dm7
G7
C
Dm7
G7
C7
F
C
C
Dm7
G7
C
Dm7
G7
C7
F
C
E7
A7
D7
G7
C

Dm7
G7
C
Dm7
G7
C7
F
C
C
Dm7
G7
C
Dm7
G7
C7
F
3
3
C
3
C
Dm7
G7
C
Dm7
G7
C7
F
C
E7
A7

D7
G7
3
C
Dm7
G7
C
Dm7
G7
3
C7
3
F
C
3
C
Dm7
G7
C
Dm7
G7
3
C7
F
C
C
Dm7
G7
C
Dm7
G7
C7
3
F

C
E7
A7
D7
G7
C
Dm7
G7
C
Dm7
G7
C7
F
C
C
3
PIANO SOLO
127
KICKS
C
Dm7
G7
C
PIANO SOLO
32
KICKS
C

Dm7
G7
C
Alto Break
Alto Sax
4
C7
F
C
C
Alto Sax
3
C7
F
C
E7
Alto Sax
3
D7
G7
Alto Sax
3
C7
F
C
C
Alto Sax
3

C7
F
C
C
ALTO SAX
3
C7
F
C
E7
ALTO SAX
A7
D7
G7
ALTO SAX
4
C7
F
C
ALTO SAX
4
C7
F

C
C
ALTO SAX
3
C7
F
C
E7
A7
D7
ALTO SAX
G7
C
ALTO SAX
DM7
G7
C
DM7
G7
C7
F
C
DM7
G7
C

I Can't Get Started with You

EM7 A7#11 DMAJ7 BM7

EM9 Gb7 F7 E7#9 Eb7#11

DMAJ7 BM7 B7b9 EM7 A7b9

DMAJ7 C9 DMAJ7 F#M9 B7b9

F#M9 B7b9 B7#9 EMAJ7 F#M7

EMAJ9/G# EMAJ9 EM7 A7#11 B7

EM7 A7#9 F#M7 B7b9

E7b5
A7b9
LAY BACK
DMAJ7
BM7
EM7
A7b9
F#9
F7
E9#11
Eb9#11
DMAJ7
B7b9
EM7
A7b9
F#M7b5
LAY BACK
B7b5(#9)
EM7b5
LAY BACK
A7b5
♩ = 75
RUBATO
EbMAJ9
DMAJ9

It Don't Mean a Thing
(If It Ain't Got That Swing)

Words and Music by
Duke Ellington and Irving Mills

Am7
D7
G
E7
3
Dizzy Solo
Am
F7
E7
Am
Dm7
G7
C
E7
Am
F7
E7
Am
Dm7
G7
C
Gm7
C7
F

Am7 D7 G

E7 Am

F7 E7 Am Dm7

G7 C

Am F7 E7

Am Dm7 G7

C E7 Am

F7 E7 Am Dm7

G7
C
Gm7
C7
F
Am7
D7
G
E7
Am
F7
E7
Am
Dm7
G7
C
Am
F7
E7
Am
Dm7
G7
C

E7
Am
F7
E7
Am
Dm7
G7
C
Gm7
C7
F
Am7
D7
G
E7
Am
F7
E7
Am
Dm7
G7
C
Am

F7
E7
Am
Dm7
G7
3
C
E7
Am
F7
E7
Am
Dm7
G7
3
C
Gm7
C7
F
Am7
3
D7
3
G
E7
Dm
F7
E7
Am
Dm7

G7 C Am

F7 E7 Am Dm7

G7 C E7

3

Am F7 E7 Am

Dm7 G7 C

Gm7 C7 F

3

Am7 D7

G E7 Am

F7
E7
Am
Dm7
G7
C
Tenor Sax Solo
128
Piano Solo
64
Bass Solo
32
Drum Solo
32
Open
Am
F7
E7
Am
Tenor Sax
4
Am
F7
E7
Am
Tenor Sax
3
Gm7
C7
F
Tenor Sax
4
Am

F7
E7
Am
Tenor Sax
3
Am
F7
E7
Am
Tenor Sax
4
Am
F7
E7
Am
3
Tenor Sax
3
Gm7
3
C7
F
3
3
Tenor Sax
3
Am
F7
E7
Tenor Sax
5
Vamp 'til Cue
Am
Cup Mute
Last Time
Trumpet
Tenor Sax

JAMBO

BY JOHN "DIZZY" GILLESPIE
AND LORRAINE GILLESPIE

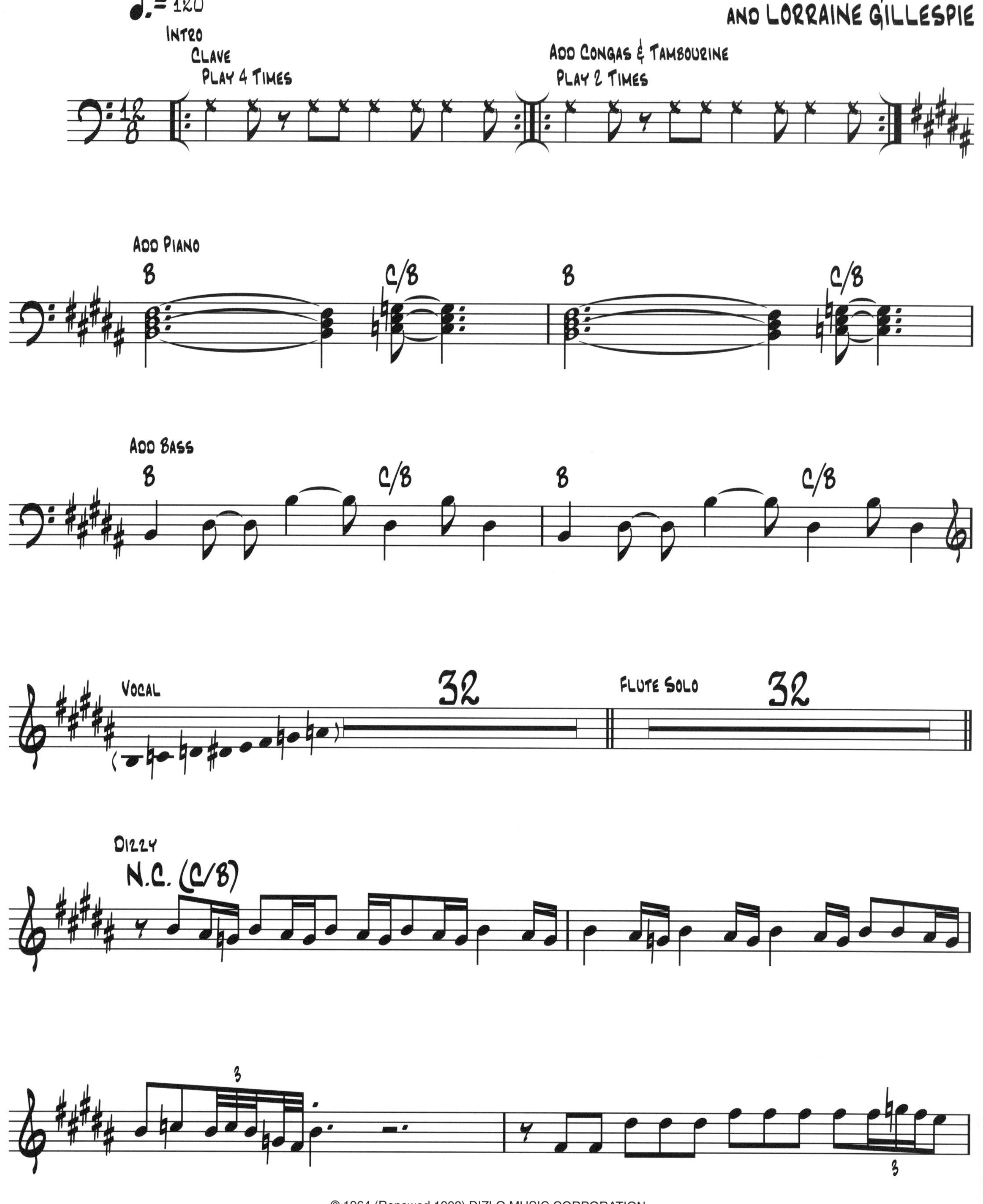

3

3

3

3

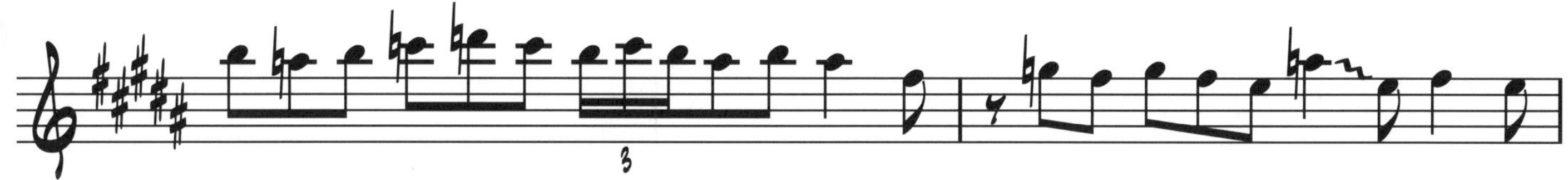
3

54

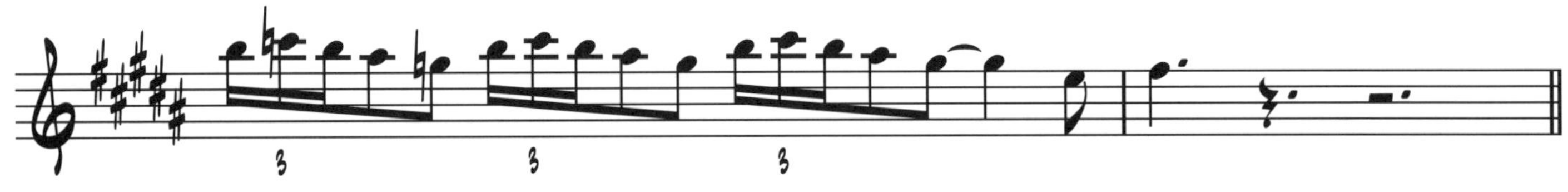

SALT PEANUTS

BY JOHN "DIZZY" GILLESPIE
AND KENNY CLARKE

D7
G G/B C C♯o
G/D
G G/B C C♯o
G/D
INTERLUDE
G
AM7 D7 G AM7 D7
G CM G
ALTO SAX
G G/B C C♯o G/D
DIZZY SING: SALT PEA-NUTS SALT PEA-NUTS
G G/B C C♯o G/D
SALT PEA - NUTS
1 SALT PEA-NUTS
2 SALT PEA-NUTS

B7 BIRD 3 E7 3

A7 3

D7 3 3 G G/B

C C#o G/D SALT PEA - NUTS SALT PEA - NUTS G G/B

C C#o G/D SALT PEA - NUTS SALT PEA - NUTS RHYTHM SECTION 8

PIANO BREAK 2 PIANO SOLO 32 ALTO SOLO 32

Alto Sax
Dizzy
Alto Sax
Dizzy Break
3
G
Am7
D7
G
3
3
Am7
D7
G7
C
G
G
Am7
D7
G
Am7
D7
G7
C
G
B7

E7
A7
D7
G
Am7
D7
3
G
Am7
D7
G7
C
G
3
Drums
22
Trumpet
Alto Sax
SALT
PEA - NUTS
SALT PEA-NUTS

Jersey Bounce

G7♭13
G7
SAXES
CMAJ9
D7
G9
CMAJ9
A♭9
CMAJ9
G7♯11(♭13)
CMAJ9
D9
SAX SOLO
2
WOODWINDS
CMAJ9
D♯07
DM7
G7
CMAJ9
D9
SAX SOLO
2
WOODWINDS
CMAJ13
BRASS
GM7
C7
PIANO INTERLUDE
FM9
B♭7
PIANO INTERLUDE
WOODWINDS

Ebm9
Ab7
Piano Interlude
Woodwinds
G7
Brass
Guitar Solo
4
Cmaj7
G7
Cmaj7
Brass
3
C9
C7 Woodwinds
Trumpet Solo
Fmaj7
G7
C9
7
Fmaj9/A
Ab7
Gm7
C7#9
Fmaj7
G7

C9
Fmaj9/A
Ab7
Fmaj9
Cm9
Woodwinds
F7
Bbm7
Eb13
G#m9
C#13
C#9
C7
tr
Brass
Fmaj9
G13
Woodwinds
C13
Fmaj9
Piano Interlude
3
Woodwinds
C13
Brass
Cmaj7
Ab7
C

Manteca

By Dizzy Gillespie, Walter Gil Fuller
and Luciano Pozo Gonzales

Bass and Percussion Interlude 4 C7 Trumpet with Brass Section Bb7 C7 Brass Vib.

Bb7 C7 Bb7 C7

Bb9 Ebmaj13 Ab7 G7#9 C7

Bb7 C7 Bb7 C7

Bb7 C7 Bb9 Ebmaj13 Ab7 G7#9

Sax Section Interlude 7 Trumpet Bbm7 Eb7#9

Abmaj7 Lay back Gmaj7 C#7#11 Gm7b5 C7

Dm7b5 G7 C7 Trumpet with Brass Section

Bb7
C7
Bb7
C7
Bb7
C7
Bb9
EbMAJ13
Ab7
G7#9
C7
Bass and Percussion Interlude
Sax Section Riff
C7
Bb7
EbM7
Trumpet over riff
Ab7
G7
C7
Bb7
EbM7
Ab7
G7
Sax Solo
16
Brass Section Interlude
Bb7
Eb13#11
AbMAJ7
3
C#7#11
FMAJ7#11
BbMAJ9
Brass fall
Trumpet Solo
BbM7
Eb7
AbMAJ7

BM7
C#7b5
G7b5
LAY BACK
C7#11
5
D7b5
3
G7#9(#11)
C7
TRUMPET WITH BRASS SECTION
Bb7
C7
Bb7
C7
Bb7
C7
Bb9
EbMAJ13
Ab7
G7#9
C7
BRASS RIFF
SIM.
BASS AND PERCUSSION RIFF
DECRESC. TO END
DRUM FILL ENDING
2

A Night in Tunisia

D7
Gmaj7
B9
F13#11
Em9(maj7)
F13#11
Em9(maj7)
F13#11
Em9(maj7)
F#m7b5
B7b5
Em13(maj7)
Sax Interlude
6
A7#11
Am(maj7)
D13b9
Gmaj7
F13#11
Em9(maj7)
F13#11

EM9(MAJ7) F13#11 EM9(MAJ7)

F#M7b5 B7b5 EM13(MAJ7) F13#11

EM9(MAJ7) F13#11 EM9(MAJ7)

F13#11 3 EM9(MAJ7) F#M7b5 B7b5

EM13(MAJ7) BM7b5 E7b9

AM7 B°7 AM13 D7

GMAJ7 6 6

B9 9 F13#11 3 EM9(MAJ7)

F13♯11
Em9(maj7)
F13♯11
Em9(maj7)
F♯m7b5
B7b5
Em9(maj7)
Interlude - Sax/Guitar
6
Sax Solo
16
Vibes Solo
7
w/Mute
F13♯11
Em9(maj7)
F13♯11
Lay back
Em9(maj7)
F13♯11
Em9(maj7)
Rubato ♩ = 70
F♯m7b5
F7/C
F7
Em13(maj7)

Rose Room

Words by Harry Williams
Music by Art Hickman

Break
F7
5
3
Time
C7
3
Cm7
F7
Bb
Fm7
Bb7
Eb
Ebm7
Ab7
Bb
G7
C7
Cm7
F7
Alto Sax Break
Bb
Alto Solo & Announcement
32
Tenor Sax Solo
6
Fade out

Sophisticated Lady

Words and Music by Duke Ellington,
Irving Mills and Mitchell Parish

CM Ab7 G7 Gb7 F7 Bb

Bb7 A7 Ab7 G7 C7 CM7 F7

Bb BM7b5 E7 A F#M7

BM7 E7 A G7 F#7

BM7 E7 A F#M7

BM7 E7 A7 DM7

B7 Bb G7 CM Ab7 G7 Gb7 F7

Bb
Bb7
A7
Ab7
G7
C7
Cm7
F7
Bb
G7#9/F
C7/F
F7#9
Bb
Bb+
Bb6
(A7)
Cadenza
Dm7
Free Time
N.C.
Slower
Rit.
Bbmaj7

TIN TIN DEO

BY WALTER GIL FULLER
AND LUCIANO POZO GONZALES

Gm
Em7b5
Am7b5
D7
3
3
Gm
Bb7
Ebmaj7
D7
Gm7
C7
3
3
F
Eb7
D7#9
Gm
3
D7#9
1/2 VALVE
Gm
Cm7
TRPT.
TEN.
F13
Bbmaj7
Cm7
F13
A7#9
D7
Gm

D7#9
FM
1/2 VALVE

D7#9
GM
3

VIBES SOLO
15
D7b5

GM(MAJ7)
3

D7#5
3
3

GM(MAJ7)
3
D7b5
pp

GM(MAJ7)
VAMP AND FADE
4

STARDUST

WORDS BY MITCHELL PARISH
MUSIC BY HOAGY CARMICHAEL

G13 Ab13 G13 Ab7#11

Fmaj9 Dm13

Ab9 G7b9 Cmaj9 Em7b5 A7b13

Dm13 A7b13 Dm13 G13

Ab9 G7#9 Cmaj9

C/G A7b13 Dm13 G7b13

Cmaj9 C7#5 F Fm7 C/G B7b9 Em7b5 Cmaj9

Stella by Starlight

(from the Paramount Picture THE UNINVITED)

Words by NED WASHINGTON
Music by VICTOR YOUNG

F#m7b5
B7
Em7b5
A7
Dm7b5
G7
C
BASS SOLO
95
DIZZY SOLO
F#m7b5
3
B7
Dm7
G7
Gm7
C7
F
Bb7
3
C
F#m7b5
B7

Em Am7 D7 G
F#m7b5 B7 Bm7b5 E7
A7 Dm7
Bb7
C F#m7b5
B7 Em7b5 A7
Dm7b5 G7 C

F#m7b5
B7
Dm7
G7
Gm7
C7
F
Bb7
C
F#m7b5
B7
Em
Am7
D7
G
Fm7b5
B7
Bm7b5
E7
A7
D7

G7
C
F#m7b5
B7
Em7b5
A7
Dm7b5
G7
C
F#m7b5
B7
Dm7
G7
Gm7
C7
F
Bb

C
F#m7b5
B7
Em
Am7
D7
G
F#m7b5
B7
Bm7b5
E7
A7
Dm7
Bb7
C
F#m7b5
B7
Em7b5
A7
Dm7b5
G7
C

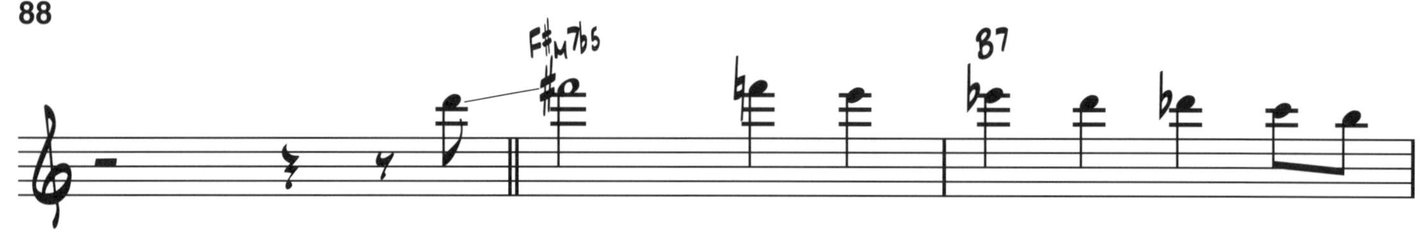
F#m7b5
B7

Dm7
G7
Gm7

C7
F

Bb
C
F#m7b5
B7

Em
Am7
D7
G
F#m7b5
B7

Bm7b5
E7
A7

D7

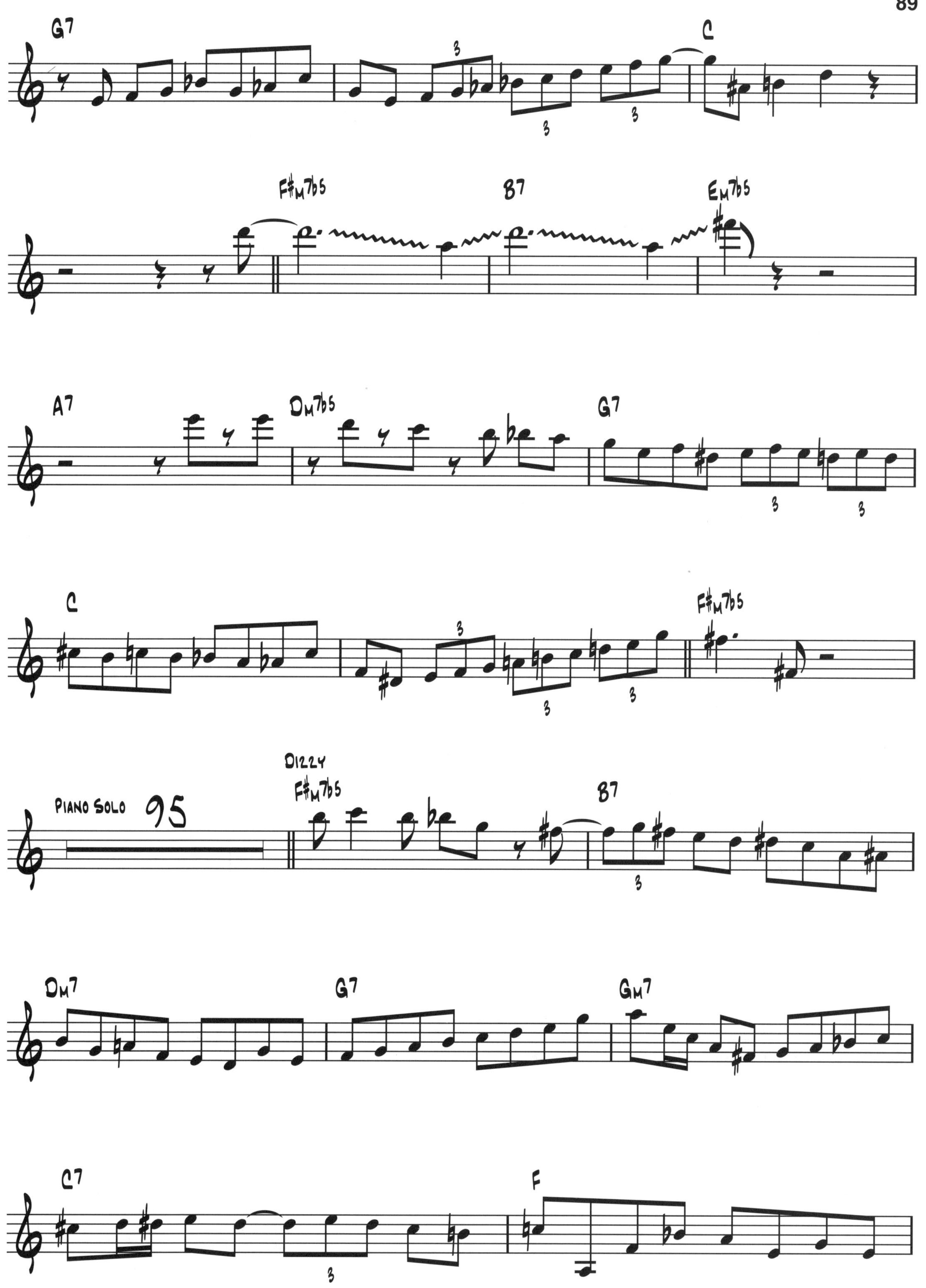
G7
C
F#m7b5
B7
Em7b5
A7
Dm7b5
G7
C
F#m7b5
PIANO SOLO 95
DIZZY
F#m7b5
B7
Dm7
G7
Gm7
C7
F

Bb7
C
Drums
7
A7
D7
G7
C
Drums
7
F#m7b5
B7
Dm7
G7
Gm7
C7
F
Bb7
Drums
7

A7
D7
3
G7
C
Drums
8
Head Out
F#m7b5
B7
Dm7
G7
Gm7
C7
F
Bb7
C
Fm7b5
B7
Em
Am7
D7
G
3
F#m7b5
B7

Bm7b5
E7
A7
D7
G7
C
F#m7b5
B7
Em7b5
A7
Dm7b5
G7
C
TAG

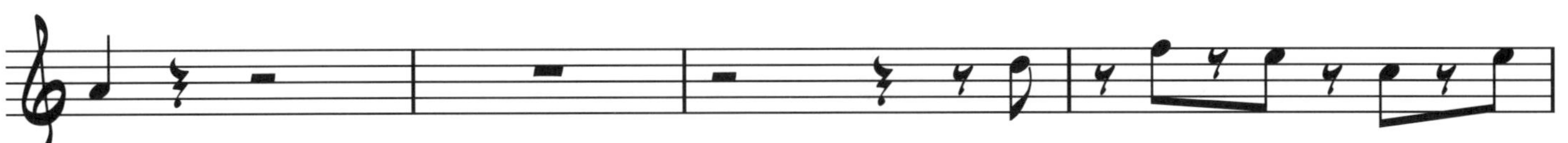

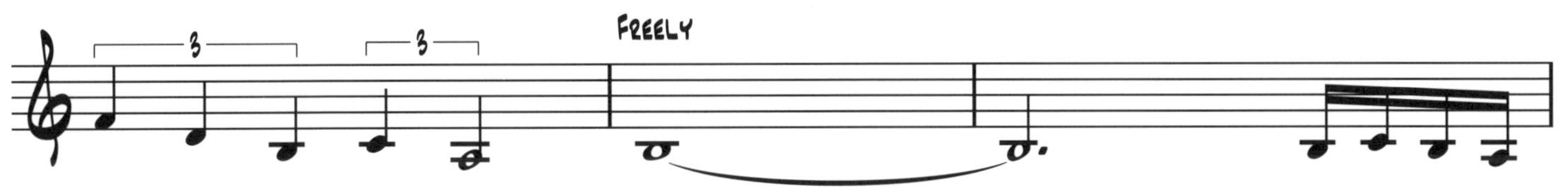
FREELY

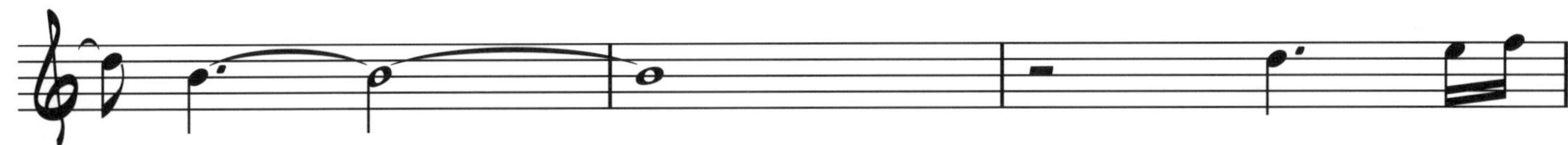

Tour de Force

By John "Dizzy" Gillespie

Fm7 Bb13b9 Ebmaj7 Fm7 Bb13b9
Ebmaj7 Ab9 Gm7 C7 Fmaj9
Gm7 Gbm7 Fm7 WOODWINDS Em7b5 Ebm7
Dm7 Dbm7 Cm7 Dm7 Dbm7
Em7b5 Ebm7 Dm7 Dbm7 Cm7 F7
Bbmaj7 Em7b5 Ebm7 Dm7 Dbm7 TRUMPET WITH BRASS
Cm7 F7 F7#11 Bbmaj7

Bbm7 Gbm7 Dbmaj9/F Dbm7b9/E Ebm7 Dm7 Dbm7 Cm7 Em7b5
Ebm7 Bbmaj9/D Bbmaj9/F Cm7 B7#11 Bbmaj7
PIANO SOLO 16
BRASS
Fm7 Bb7#9 Ebmaj7 Gb7
Fm7 Bb7b9 Ebmaj7 Ebmaj7 C7 Fmaj9 F#o7
TRUMPET SOLO
Gm7 C7 F7 Em7b5 Ebm7
LAY BACK
Dm7 LAY BACK
Dbm7 C7 F7
Bbmaj7 Dbm7b5 Em7b5 Ebm7

Dm7 Dbm7 Cm7 F7 Bbmaj7
Em7b5 Ebm7 Dm7 Dbm7 Cm7 F7
Bbmaj7 Em7b5 Ebm7
Dm7 Dbm7 Cm7 F7 Bbmaj7
Em7b5 Ebm7 Dm7 Dbm7 Cm7 F7
Bbmaj7 Em7b5 Ebm7 Dm7 Dbm7
Cm7 F7 Bbmaj7 Fm7 Bb7b9

Ebmaj7 F#o7 Fm7 5 Bb7b9
Ebmaj7 Gm7 C7
Fm7 F#o7 Gm7 C7b9 Fm9
Em7b5 Ebm7 Dm7 Dbm7 Cm7 F7
Bbmaj7 Em7b5 Dbm7 Dm7 Dbm7 3
Cm7 Bbmaj7 Em7b5 Ebm7
Brass
3
Dm7 Dbm7 Cm7 F7 Bbmaj7 Gb7 F7 3

Em7b5
SAX SOLO
18
WOODWINDS
Em7b5 Ebm7
Dm7 Dbm7 Cm7 F7 Dm7 Dbm7
Em7b5 Ebm7 Dm7 Dbm7 Cm7
Bbmaj7 Bb7 Em7b5 Ebm7 Dm7 Dbm7
Cm7 Dm7 Dbm7 Em7b5 Ebm7
Dm7 Dbm7 Cm7 Bbmaj7
BRASS
Em7b5
Ebm7 Dm7 Cm7 B7b5 Bm(maj7) Bbmaj13#11

WOODYN' YOU

BY DIZZY GILLESPIE

Bbm9
Eb7#9
Abmaj7
Cm9
F7
Cm9
F7
Cm9
F7#9
Bbmaj7
Am7b5
D7#9
Gm7b5
C7#9
Fm7b5
Bb7#9
Ebmaj7
Am7b5
D7#9
Gm7b5
C7#9
Fm7b5
Bb7#9
Ebmaj7
Am7b5
D7#9

GM7b5
C7#9
FM7b5
Bb7#9
EbMAJ7
SAX SOLO
14
TRUMPET SOLO
AM7b5
D7#9
GM7b5
C7#9
FM7b5
Bb7#9
EbMAJ7
AM7b5
D7#9
GM7b5
C7#9
FM7b5
Bb7#9
EbMAJ7

Bbm9 Eb7 Bbm9 Eb7 Bbm9 Eb7#9
Abmaj7 Cm9 F7
Cm9 F7 Cm7 F13b9
Bb13b9 Am7b5 D7#9
Gm7b5 C7#9 Fm7b5
Bb7#9 Ebmaj7
SAX
Am7b5 D7#9 Gm7b5
C7#9 Fm7b5 Bb7#9

E♭maj7
Am7b5
D7#9
Gm7b5
C7#9
Fm7b5
Bb7#9
E♭maj7
SAX INTERLUDE
8
SAX
Am7b5
D7#9
Gm7b5
C7#9
Fm7b5
Bb7#9
E♭maj7
Fm7b5
MOLTO RIT.
Bb7#9
E♭maj7